HORSE — 30 MILES (48 KM) PER HOUR

SKATEBOARD — 15 MILES (24 KM) PER HOUR

DOG — 20 MILES (32 KM) PER HOUR

NEW HORIZONS — 36,373 MILES (58,536 KM) PER HOUR

NOW THAT'S FAST!: NEW HORIZONS

JACKRABBIT — 45 MILES (72 KM) PER HOUR

HUMAN — 12 MILES (19 KM) PER HOUR

BICYCLE — 15 MILES (24 KM) PER HOUR

NOW THAT'S FAST!

NEW HORIZONS

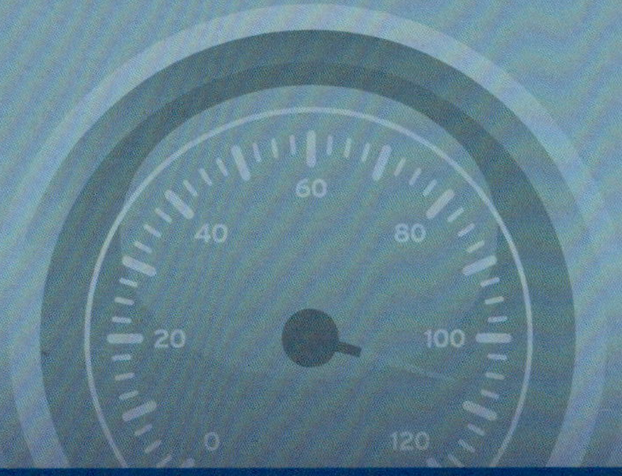

KATE RIGGS

CREATIVE EDUCATION • CREATIVE PAPERBACKS

Published by Creative Education and
Creative Paperbacks
P.O. Box 227, Mankato, Minnesota 56002
Creative Education and Creative Paperbacks
are imprints of The Creative Company
www.thecreativecompany.us

Design by Blue Design;
production by Dana Cheit
Art direction by Rita Marshall
Printed in the United States of America

Photographs by Alamy (NASA Photo, Science Photo Library), Creative Commons Wikimedia (NASA, NASA/Bill Ingalls, NASA/JHUAPL/SwRI, NASA/Kim Shiflett), Getty Images (Matt Stroshane/Stringer/Getty Images News, Universal History Archive/Universal Images Group), NASA (JHUAPL/SwRI, NASA/JHUAPL/SwRI, NASA/JHUAPL/SwRI/Carlos Hernandez)

Library of Congress Cataloging-in-Publication Data
Names: Riggs, Kate, author.
Title: New Horizons / Kate Riggs.
Series: Now that's fast!
Includes bibliographical references and index.
Summary: A fast-paced, high-interest overview of the features, purpose, history, and high-speed capabilities of the New Horizons probe—one of the fastest-moving spacecraft in history.
Identifiers: ISBN 978-1-64026-033-7 (hardcover) / ISBN 978-1-62832-588-1 (pbk) / ISBN 978-1-64000-062-9 (eBook)
This title has been submitted for CIP processing under LCCN 2018944092.

CCSS: RI.1.1, 2, 4, 5, 6, 7; RI.2.2, 5, 6, 7, 10; RI.3.1, 5, 7, 8; RF.1.1, 3, 4; RF.2.3, 4

First Edition HC 9 8 7 6 5 4 3 2 1
First Edition PBK 9 8 7 6 5 4 3 2 1

Table of Contents

PROBING SPACE

A robotic craft that explores outer space is called a probe. Powerful rockets send probes into space. An Atlas V rocket made *New Horizons* go about 36,000 miles (57,936 km) per hour!

NEW HORIZONS
NASA

New Horizons launched in 2006. Scientists built it to fly past Pluto. They wanted to learn more about that icy dwarf planet. It is so far out in the **solar system** that we hardly knew anything about it.

GENERATING POWER

New Horizons is shaped like a grand piano. It is made out of thin layers of **aluminum**. Sticking out from the body is a **generator**. It has a heat source that makes electricity. This powers the probe without having to charge it like a battery. On the flat side of the probe is a dish antenna.

Mission Operation
JOHNS HOPKINS
NEW HORIZONS
NEW HORIZONS

SENDING MESSAGES

People control *New Horizons* from Earth. The probe sends back information using **radio waves**. These waves took about four and a half hours to reach Earth from Pluto.

GROUP PROJECT

The craft was built in Maryland. It arrived at Florida's Kennedy Space Center in 2005. Dr. Alan Stern leads the mission team of scientists. Other groups around the United States work with NASA on different parts of the project.

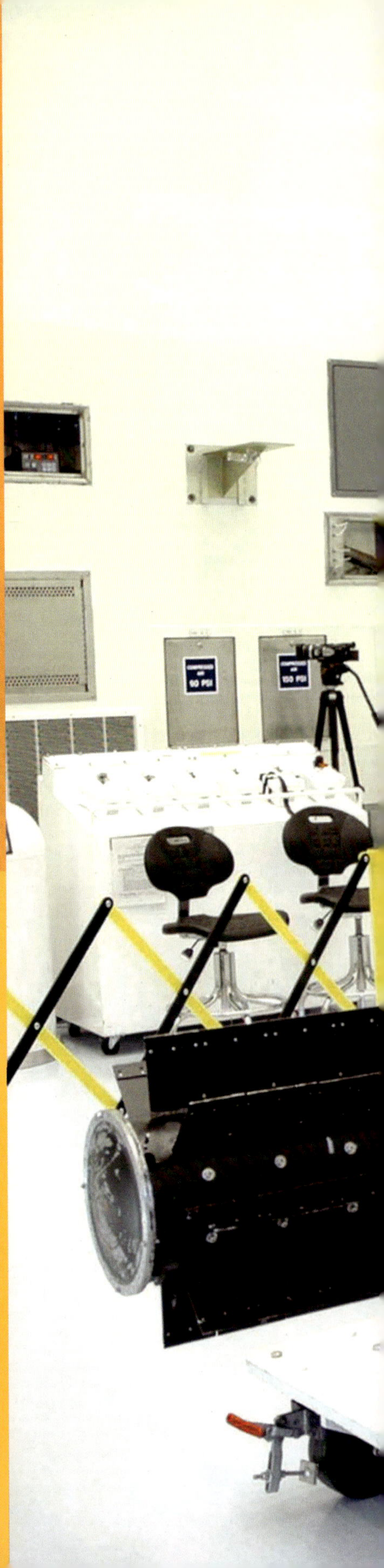

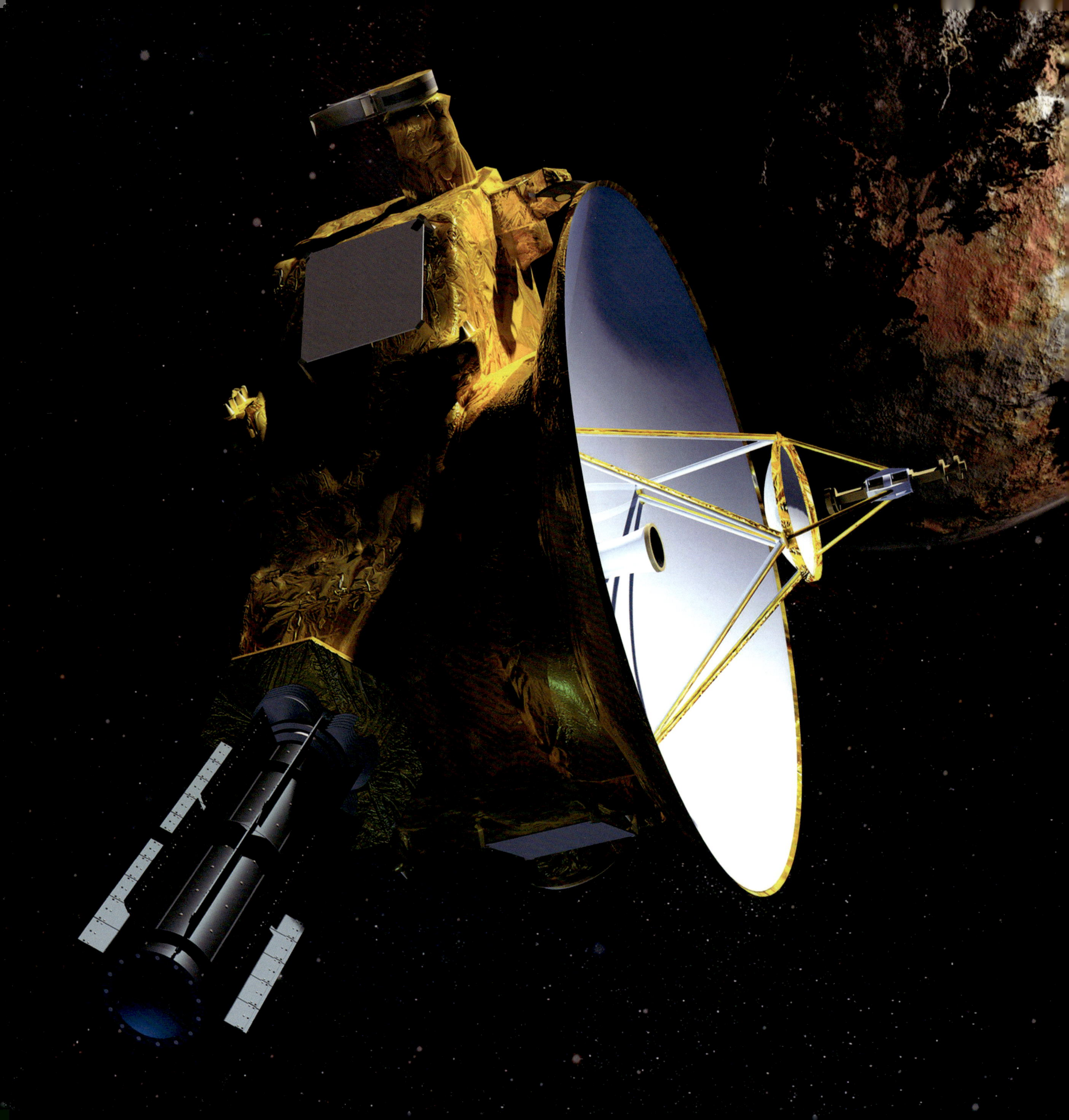

New Horizons travels through space at more than 31,000 miles (49,890 km) per hour. It cannot slow down. Its cameras take pictures quickly.

PLANETARY PICTURES

New Horizons flew past Pluto in 2015. It took 15 months for all the data to reach Earth! People could finally see the first clear pictures of Pluto after that.

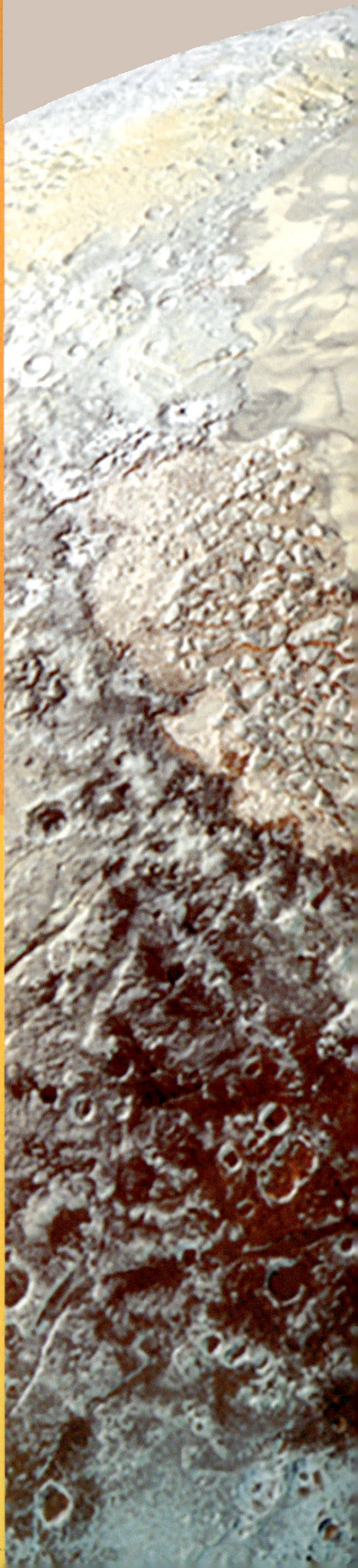

Mission controllers on Earth guide *New Horizons*. It is flying to other distant, icy objects. These are in the **Kuiper belt**. In January 2019, it should fly by an object called 2014 MU69.

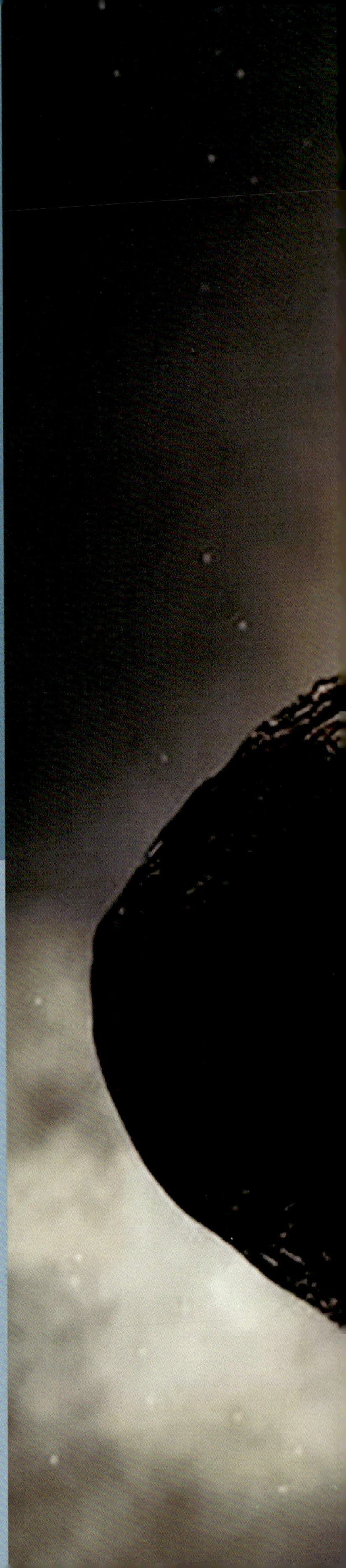

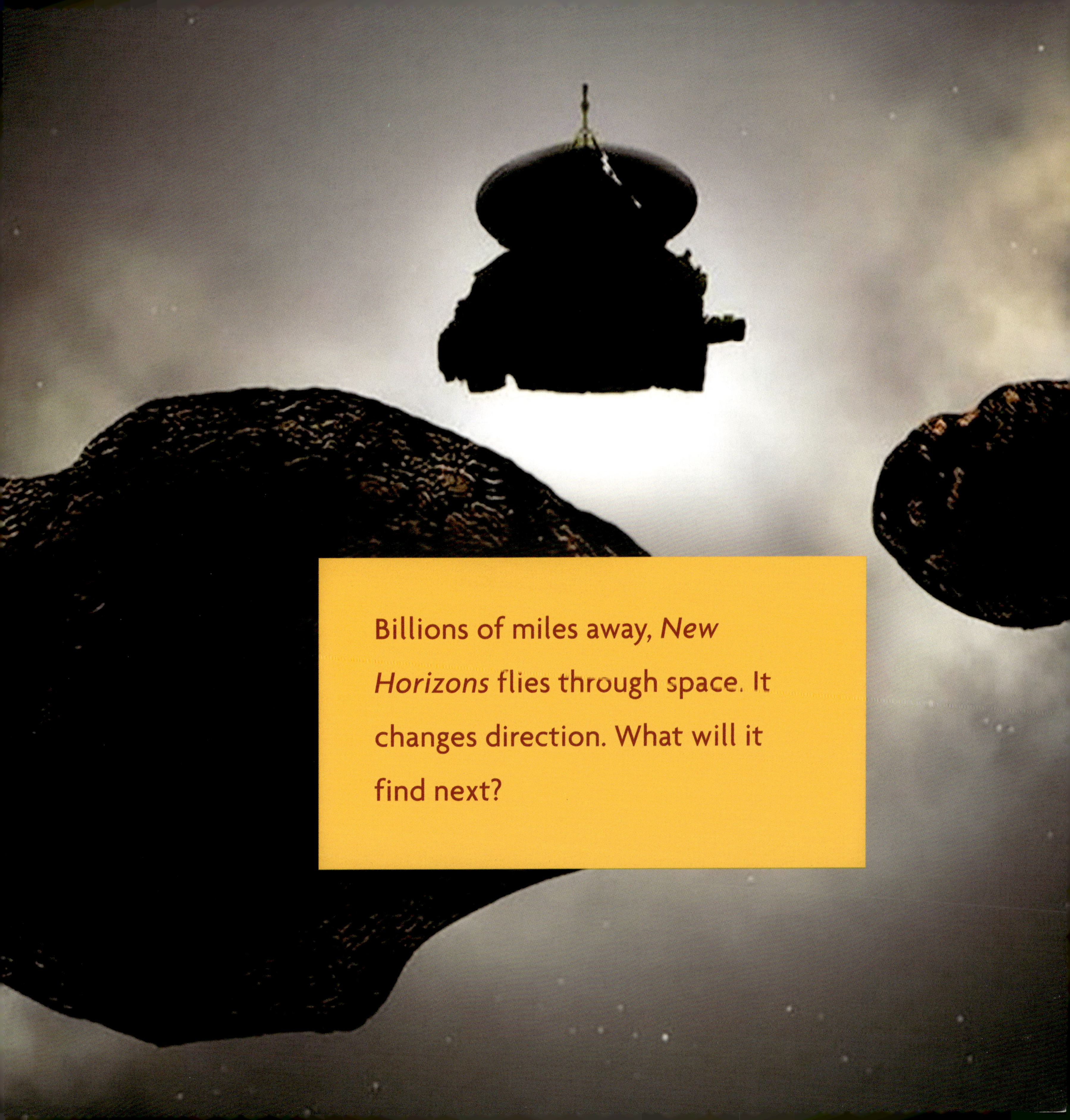

Billions of miles away, *New Horizons* flies through space. It changes direction. What will it find next?

BREAKING DOWN *NEW HORIZONS*

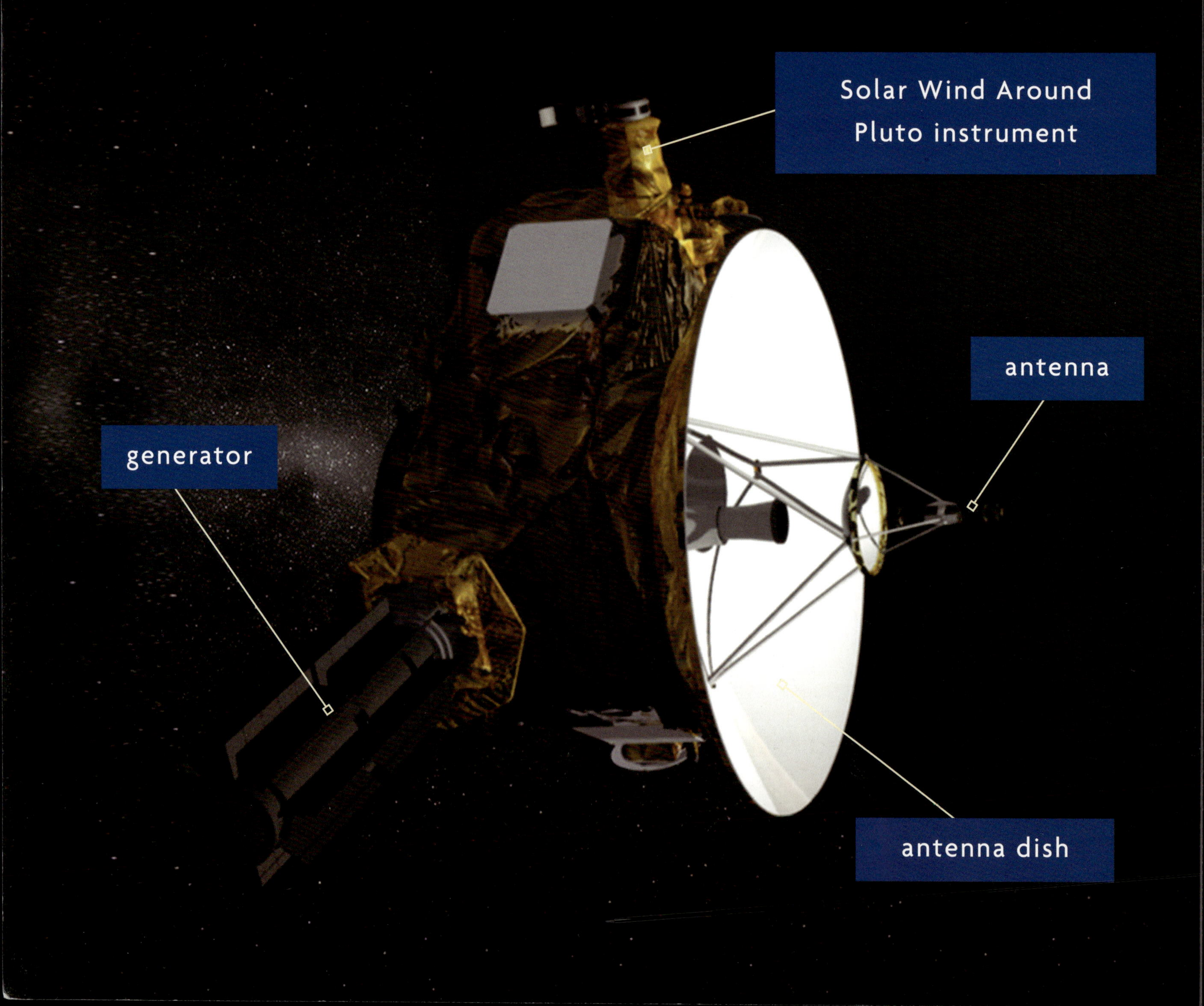

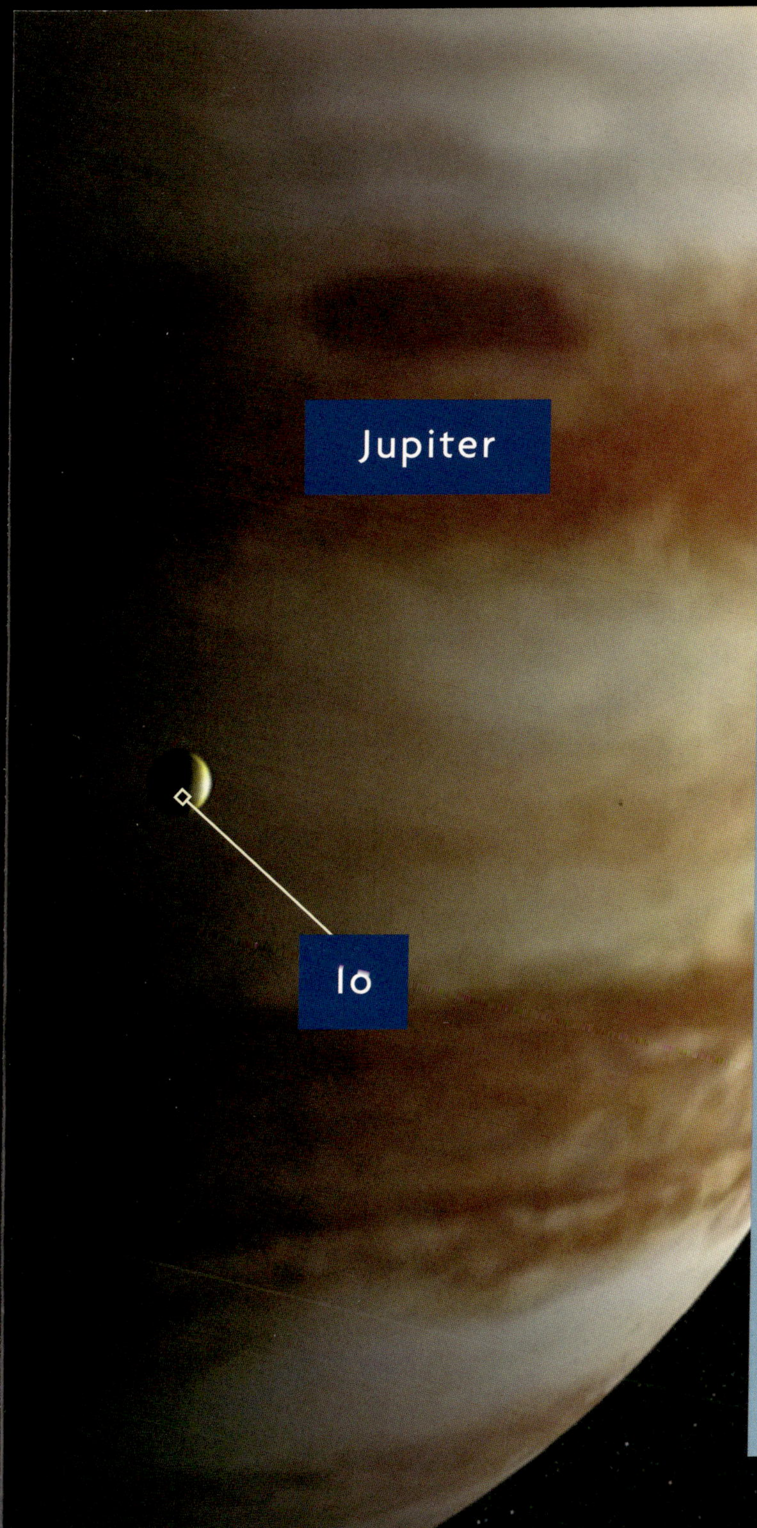

Fast Facts

The body of *New Horizons* is almost 2.5 feet (0.8 m) thick.

The Atlas V rocket that launched *New Horizons* used five **solid rocket boosters**.

Four of the seven instruments on *New Horizons* measure different atmospheric qualities.

The antenna dish is 6.9 feet (2.1 m) wide.

Glossary

aluminum—a lightweight metal used in transportation, packaging, and many other applications

generator—a machine that turns energy into electricity

Kuiper belt—an area of the solar system beyond Neptune thought to contain many asteroids, comets, and icy bodies

radio waves—a type of energy that moves across space at the speed of light; used for long-distance communication

solar system—the sun, the planets and their moons, and smaller bodies such as asteroids and comets

solid rocket boosters—reusable rockets that help a spacecraft take off and speed up

Read More

Carson, Mary Kay. *Mission to Pluto: The First Visit to an Ice Dwarf and the Kuiper Belt.* New York: Houghton Mifflin Harcourt, 2017.

Saxena, Shalini. *Pluto and Other Dwarf Planets.* New York: Britannica Educational / Rosen Educational Services, 2017.

Index